Insight

By: Nicole Lee

Dedication

This book is dedicated… first, to the Divine God Intelligence of the Universe, the source who created me, and the one who continues to guide me along this journey. I praise and honor the Almighty Divine God Intelligence!

Secondly, to my God-given gifts, my children: Darius, Dejah, and Devin – I love you always; you are my reason for being and my inspiration of why I do what I do! Thank you for keeping me grounded. The responsibility of parenting allows one to experience unconditional love. My children are my power base. My responsibility as a mother is to teach and nurture these Divine Beings who God has put me in charge of. As time consuming as children are, they need to be inspired and encouraged at all times. Sacrificial offering = your time.

Mothers who are home with their children have the power to feed into their children's expanding powers. This power dwells within their spirit. A mother has the power to pour into her children when their spirit is in need of light. Woman is the sub-conscious mind of God. Children nowadays come here with a knowing that they are destined to be great and mothers are their first teacher. I thank the Divine for trusting me with my gifts; through obedience to the Almighty Divine God; Darius, Dejah and Devin, the BEST is yet to come yaw, Ase!!!

To ALL Mothers: Go home to your children and nurture them with unconditional love and watch GOD bless you beyond measures!! Ase.

Testimonial

"Nicole Lee's writing plays a huge part of my everyday life. Her writings have given me so much inspiration, motivation, hope and courage. One of the best messages I received from her writings, is 'to never let fear occupy your mind'. Nicole's writings are good for EVEYONE to read. It teaches self-motivation, hope, healing, businesses, positive affirmations, and spiritual guidance. I give much thanks to Nicole Lee for writing such amazing books and for her inspiring me to live my dreams. Thanks for helping me along my journey!"

~Tamika O.

Book of Insight

Introduction

Insight came into fruition while blogging about my first book, *Healing Cosmetologist*. During the journey, new titles to books and articles would ignite during my dream state of being.

As I would write, the message would just flow in my mind. This writing journey is mystical and is linked to a higher source within the Universe.

God has spoken His truth to me:

"Baby girl, close down the Salon and worry not of ANY finances. You and your children WILL be cared for during this transition. I will return to you 100-fold of blessings and favor upon you and your children and children's children in generational favor; if only you would position yourself as a FULLTIME mom and begin writing books of your knowledge so that you will be financially, emotionally, and physically successful by way of your THOUGHTS. Intellectual property is the highest commodity."

So, here's book #2, *Insight*. *Insight* is composed of short stories about how to ignite blissful living. These short stories are my personal testimonies of how I FINALLY found a joy within my spirit without anything external. Love, joy, and peace comes from within. Your inner self must be whole in order to live a blissful life. The physical self is temporary; the spiritual self is eternal. Once you capture the essence of your truest self, which is spirit, life as a physical being becomes as eternal as spirit; it becomes a marriage with self - whole, pure, and enlightened!

Insight 1:

"Release the Slave Mentality Energy"

Chakra - the Sanskrit (ancient Indian language) word refers to the seven wheels of spiritual power in the human body—starting from the base of the spine to the top of the head that regulates emotions.

To most, the word 'chakra' is taboo and seems to place fear in those who do not understand.

With much prayer, research, and study, I discovered that since the Chakra System regulates emotions, it is linked to unraveling slave mentality. In this sense, a slave is one who obeys someone else's thoughts and beliefs instead of their own. Deep embedded emotions that dwell within us, at a cellular level, have a major effect on our thinking and they play a huge part in creating a slave mentality. When one has an understanding about the Chakra System, it can become a tool to use to unravel negative emotions and free you from the slavery mindset.

When one researches and studies Chakras while walking in their God-given purpose, God has a way of allowing you to explore His awesome wonders of the world. GOD is EVERYWHERE. I no longer put God in a box.

God has a way of connecting you to key people along your journey for support, confirmation, and guidance.

My first interaction with the Chakra System was during a spiritual journey to Sedona, Arizona. In my opinion, Sedona, Arizona is one of the most powerful energy centers of the world. The positive energy that is surrounded by red rock mountains and a familiarity of being ignited with an understanding of GOD and His awesome wonders!

Through more research and an open mind, I realized that the Chakra System can be reached anywhere, from the "Book of Revelation" in the Bible to the greatest band of all time, Earth, Wind & Fire!

In the "Book of Revelation" there are seven churches. The body of Christ is you, NOT a building. The seven churches /candlesticks are related to the seven energy centers in the body. Once these energy centers are clear and aligned, you become a beam of light from within that exudes out! This is what you call the resurrection of Christ consciousness.

Earth, Wind & Fire, one of the world's favorite bands, have been trying to bring forth awareness about the Chakra System for years. On their album, *Powerlight*, there's even a full picture of the Chakra System. Earth, Wind & Fire's music speaks spirituality! Their songs, music, and words speak love, joy, peace, humanity, and of the spirit. If you have ever been to one of their concerts, you most likely felt the energy in the atmosphere!

The Chakra System is connected to the elements of earth, air, water, and fire. Each of these elements exist within every cell of our body.

I was amazed how this one word is connected to EVERYTHING!

Here's an excerpt from my 1st published book *Healing Cosmetologist* that offers more insight about the Chakra System:

"We are physical beings having human experiences. The physical body is a vehicle to move and operate in this Earthly realm. The human body is a combination of organs, blood, vessels, cells, your spirit (which is your true self), and ENERGY(Chakra).

The space between the physical body and your spirit is an ENERGY field called CHAKRA. There are seven (7) main Chakras in the body that control energy flow:

-Root Chakra- is related to issues related to survival and material needs.
-Sacral Chakra- is related to issues related to physical desires/addiction.
-Solar Plexus- is related to issues related to power and control.
-Heart Chakra- is related to issues related to love.
-Throat Chakra- is related to issues about speaking your truth.
-Third Eye Chakra- is related to intuition.
-Crown Chakra- is related to receiving direct thoughts from the Divine God."

~ Healing Cosmetologist

Everything we need here on earth to operate successfully, dwells deep within. Seeking the treasures within allows us to experience the treasures provided for us here on earth. This is how we experience: "On earth as it is in heaven".

I encourage you to seek truth with guidance from the highest power energy source, God, and watch Him unravel the awesome wonders He has for you!

EVERYTHING is connected!

"Release the Slave Mentality Energy"
Notes:

Insight 2:

"God, Self, Family Then Business"

There is a formula to TRUE prosperity, abundance, and success: God + Self + Family + Business = True SUCCESS!

God, who is the Creator of ALL things that are good, has given us the ability to become great. Our greatness manifests when we walk in the alignment of our purpose in life. Prioritizing our lives to the things that truly matter is key to aligning ourselves to receive the blessings God has for us.

Placing God in the equation as first, sets the tone for what's next in line. Placing self as the next importance allows God to pour His energy of love, joy, peace, and intelligence into you so that you may duplicate that in others. Family, whether it is your parents, siblings, spouse, children, or loyal friends, placing them next in the equation will allow you to see what God has planted in you as you pour into them.

During the creation of this foundation, God then pours His Favor upon you because you understand and apply the mathematics of His Universe. The desires of your heart manifest instantaneously because you asked. In manifesting your heart's desires, God will guide you and send people your way to help you achieve the desires of your heart.

Faith without works is dead.

The abundance of blessings from God comes in many forms: monetary and generational favor, just to name a few.

Monetary abundance allows all needs and desires to be met. This also allows one to help others in need and develop Empires. In my experience, I've discovered that as a Parent, Children are the power base of your being. Children need to be inspired and encouraged at ALL times. Sacrificial offering? YOUR TIME. Your children are the reason of WHY the manifestation of your Empire even exists!

To acquire a great Empire, it is required that one pours their most valuable knowledge to those who love and support them!"

OVERALL…

Not only is a supportive foundation required, having an Entrepreneurial mindset is necessary. When you begin to REALIZE the knowledge that you've acquired during adulthood is valuable, you then have recognized that:

"Intellectual Property is the Highest Commodity!"

Remember:

1. Be a doer.

2. Turn thought into action

3. DISCIPLINE yourself

"Do not be arrogant. By being arrogant, you admit to the world that you are scared but are not able to acknowledge this. By being humble, you admit to your daily fears, but you fight through these and in the process, you create true friendships."

~Brad Snyder 1994 #houseofcigars

God has placed everything we need inside of our being to accomplish our destiny. Aligning and prioritizing our life to the things that truly matter is the SUCCESS.

Putting God first, then taking care of self allows one to pour life and good energy into family and then business. This equation manifests the peace of God which passeth ALL understanding to keep our minds in perfect peace.

"God, Self, Family Then Business"
Notes:

Insight 3:

"Sexual Soul-Ties, Life Purpose, and a Queen"

"What is a sexual soul-tie? A sexual soul-tie is like a linkage in the spiritual realm between two people. The ties or the energy links their souls together, which can bring fourth either beneficial results or negative results."

~ Healing Cosmetologist

Now, I place no judgement on anyone when it comes to choosing WHO you desire to share intimacy with. Intimacy, sex, love, lust, attraction, whatever you want to call it, it's REAL and it is BEAUTIFUL...with the RIGHT one!

I adore sexual intimacy. I've always had high sexual energy from my teenage years until NOW! Yet, while maturing, I began experiencing the negative effects of the one thing I found to be energetic and very satisfying.

It all started, as a single woman, when the interactions with men became unsatisfying. I later learned it was beyond just disconnection, it was my spirit warning me not to be involved with this particular person. It's a signal of an UNEQUALLY yoked being.

Because of my awakened awareness, I began to seek and study about the energy of sex:

"The emotion of sex cannot be entirely suppressed, but it can be sublimated. It can be diverted in such a way that it becomes a truly irresistible power for action toward one's goals in life.... when the emotion of love, which is psychic, is blended with the emotion of sex, which is physical, an influence or power is generated which steps up the vibration rate of every cell in the body. These emotions are the handiwork of nature, instruments through which the Creator provided for perpetuation of life."

~ Healing Cosmetologist

From this study, I learned that sex is energy and can be used toward achieving my destiny. Also, when sex is combined with LOVE, it can be healing for both participants.

So, I thought, *wow, God truly created this practice for a reason.*

As I began to study and apply these new beliefs, my gifts became more heightened.

Discovery as the Queen I AM when it comes to sex, I discovered an AWESOME ability that ALL WOMEN have if they would just tap into their POWER and recognize who they are - we are natural born HEALERS. This is the TRUE ability of a QUEEN: "As woman, you have a gift, a power to process the needs of man by ways of sexual contact. Having this ability is rewarding for the man, God has for you, a husband."

~ Healing Cosmetologist

Queen, when you encounter with man sexually and the eruptions of his semen enters your womb, you are receiving information about him and his needs. As you absorb him, you will have the ability to: build him up, speak life into him, help him with his business or career, give him insight on his health and what it takes to keep him balanced naturally and bring light to his life. This is OUR power when used according to God the Creator of it ALL.

Now of course, this only works in a COMMITTED relationship among two people who have agreed honestly that they LOVE each other and are ONE.

As King pours himself into Queen and she gives him what he needs, he will perform much greater as King and head of his household. Kingdom man is who he will become. It's the law of cause and effect.

Here's an affirmation to speak as a tool to conquer the battle of a negative soul-tie or renew the relationship you're currently in by eliminating the residue of lingering past relationships:

"Divine God,

I call upon you to help me heal, let go, and cut the etheric cord that no longer serve my higher purpose. By the decision of my own free will, I ask you to go to the root and remove any etheric cord and loose me from every soul-tie of the dark side agents outside human form and any thought forms of negativity that I may cling to for my own physical satisfaction. I ask that all cords attached to me that are not aligned with love, light and positive intensions be released.

List the names of all sexual connections that you have encountered:

_____

_____

_____

Surround me with a healing light to protect me from future attachments from anyone else that may come along. Gift me with a strong discernment to help identify when such a spirit tries to come into my presence. I fill my heart chakra with love, light, and laughter, so it will not call the cord back. Ase!"

Now that you have spoken to the Universe about this, you will acquire a heightened sense of intuition. Women are the subconscious mind of God.

This is real talk, sometimes one must use this affirmation several times because the etheric cord is so strong; from phone calls to thoughts, to dreams.... that cord can show up anytime, anywhere.

Become aware of this; pay attention to whom you share your intimate energy with.

Awareness: After intimacy, are you energetic or drained? Do you acquire insight on your goals or are your thoughts foggy? Are your thoughts positive or negative, are you happy or sad?

This will give you insight on WHAT type of energy you are intertwining with. These auras/energies leave a spiritual residue when in sexual contact or even a kiss (all liquids are transferable). If your partner doesn't practice any type of cleansing (detox, juicing, herbal baths, daily affirmations, prayer, and meditation) you will acquire WHATEVER they embody mentally, physically, and spiritually whether it be positive or negative.

Imagine the confused aura/energy of one who has multiple sexual partners, one who is carrying MULTIPLE energies around with them.

This CONFUSION can BLOCK you from recognizing WHAT your life purpose is. This is why sexual soul-ties has an effect on your life purpose.

Knowledge is power. Just be aware. Your destiny is your blessing. Connect with someone who will assist you toward your life purpose. Allow God to guide you and pray that He will continue to cover you at your weakest moments. I truly believe God has gifted us with a purpose, a purpose to create peace on earth. Begin to desire what that purpose is and surround yourself with like-minded and like-spirited people that will be a blessing to you, not a hindrance.

"Sexual Soul-Ties, Life Purpose, and a Queen"

Notes:

Insight 4:

"Desire More Clarity?"

I have a solution as to how to acquire more clarity in your life!!!

When you ingest the proper nourishment, and think positive thoughts, you will have more clarity about your reason of being. Here is a suggestion to acquiring CLARITY:

Over a 30-day period (because it takes 30 days to create habit) practice juicing every other day. Juicing is the liquid form of receiving the proper nutrition the body TRULY desires. The combination of fresh fruits, vegetables, and herbs are key components to acquiring a healthy body, mind, and spirit.

Here are some great ingredients to use for juicing to enhance clarity: Kale, Spinach, Berries, Kiwi, Banana, Hemp Protein,

Turmeric, Flax Seed, Echinacea, Ginger, Orange Juice, or Almond Milk.

On the opposite days, eat exactly what you desire whether you think it's nutritional or not. The days you return to juicing, you're detoxing, getting rid of the foods you ate the day before, so your body is on a constant cleanse.

The days you juice is for nourishment, the days you eat whatever you "think" you desire is for pleasure.

After a few days of this process, the palette of your tongue will begin to change and your taste buds will become keener on "taste".

Foods you once enjoyed will be eliminated from your diet because you taste its true value which is 0.

A physical, mental, and spiritual transformation will begin to manifest. The days that you are juicing, your mind and your thoughts will begin to align with the Almighty

God, Creator of the Universe. Throughout your day, God will speak to you on all levels.

If you desire CLARITY, this is the perfect time to ask God whatever is on your mind and he will answer immediately!

I remember the day I ate whatever I desired, I ate some bar-b-que ribs. When I took a bite, and began to chew, my tongue alarmed me that what I was tasting was stinking, so I spit it out! I thought I was tripping; how was I able to taste the "smell" of the meat I was eating? This was an amazing discovery; I realized that I had acquired the ability to warn my body through taste NOT to ingest certain foods. During the juicing phase, I seemed to have acquired a keener ability of my six senses.

There are so many benefits to this practice: You will acquire clarity, it will heighten your sense of smell, taste, sight, hearing, touch, intuition, and it will align you with the Universe and all the gifts it has for you.

I encourage anyone who desires clarity to try this practice, it's life changing and freeing!

I desire the Abundance of God's favor, joy, love, peace and prosperity for you and your family.

"Desire More Clarity?"

Notes:

Insight 5:

"Spiritual Beings"

A spiritual being is the soul from within the physical body. Our physical body is nothing more than a vehicle. Our truest self, our core of being IS our spirit!

Before we were born, we made an agreement in the spiritual realm as a spirit to come to earth and bring forth a specific purpose.

We are all here for a reason.

As we were snuggled in our mother's womb, influences began to evolve from our mother's and father's historical imprint.

When our mother gave birth, our journey of life began.

Our influences began to evolve from whom we "should" be, based on influences (positive or negative) from our mother, father, caregivers, teachers, and friends to our own truths.

We began to mold into whom we should be by our response from these influences.

Our belief systems began to evolve based on the teachings from church or whatever our parents or caregivers believed.

In our young adult stage, our emotions began to guide our choices, from whom we fall in love with, sex, career choices, marriage and parenting.

Decisions, decisions…all these ideas and influences!

Now we're adults and our inner core is crying out! Now we begin to question, WHO am I?

Most times, we tend to base our decisions on making someone else happy and in turn have created a life that we never desired.

So now we desire change, yet we have baggage…from bills, dysfunctional relationships, children, jobs we don't care for, and the list continues.

Now what? *I'm glad you asked.*

This is a wonderful space to be in. Your inner spirit wants to come out and shine. Your inner core desires to operate as agreed the day you were born!!!

We are all here for a purpose! God has created us for greatness! Yes, all of us! We were created in the image of God, which means we are co-creators and we have the power to create!

I encourage you to seek what that purpose is. Reach deep down within, meditate, and ask God to guide and assist you in finding what that purpose is. Discovering your purpose is a process but it's rewarding when you begin to walk in it!!

I truly believe if everyone would just have the desire to walk in their purpose and truly act on it that this world we live in would become heaven on earth!

Light is what this world is moaning for. Love, joy, and peace is what we so desperately need right now!!

So, I encourage you to go within, talk with your higher source, and become the LIGHT!! No matter what your belief system is, we are all connected to the main energy source, Creator of all - God the Divine Intelligence.

I believe there is truth in all religions. I believe there are many paths to God.

We are spiritual beings having human experiences, let's begin to experience blissful living, even in a world full of chaos and darkness. Let's begin collectively and consciously to create the Garden of Eden; it is a mindset that can be created in physical form!! Heaven on earth is the desire!! Become the light of the world.

"Spiritual Beings"

Notes:

Insight 6:

"The Age of Aquarius"

In your 40's as a woman, QUEENDOMENESS should be on the arrival. If not, then you missed a lesson.

Below is a list of things that may be blocking your THINKING to make you operate less than a Queen:

- You try to mimic the people around you. You create the idea of self-based on what you see and/or feel around you. **Solution:** Go within. Be your OWN individual self. Create who you desire to be.

- You're still concerned about what people will say and/or think about you. **Solution:** Rebuke the thought of such criticism.

- Priorities are out of sync because of who you THINK you are. **Solution:** Be rid of the things that have NO value toward your purpose. Then you will begin to prioritize on purpose.

Start there and journal the results. It's a Process. This pouring out on pen allows you to unravel the Queen from within. #micdropped

"The Age of Aquarius"
Notes:

Insight 7:

"Just Relax Y'll"

Relax your mind, body, and spirit by practicing meditation. Once you master positive thinking, you'll experience a stress-free life.

Here's a suggestion: Your space must be free of any distraction of sound (TV, radio, people). Sit up straight or lay on your back.

Choose tools of your choice to assist with relaxation: speak aloud the 37th Psalm and light a lavender candle, white sage, or frankincense incense (these suggested tools assist with the clearing of any negative residue in your space).

Close your eyes. Begin to inhale for 3 counts, exhale for 6 counts. Continue this until you feel relaxed and all thoughts in your mind are silent.

This is the beginning, it's a process. It takes practice to discipline the mind. In order to be in control of your thoughts, repetition of this practice is necessary.

Breathing deeply is necessary to operate fully and be in alignment with the Universe. Breathing brings forth oxygen to the brain. Oxygen is vital for brain healing and its proper function.

So just relax y'll and breathe....

"Just Relax Y'll"
Notes:

Insight 8:

"Conquer Fear and Anxiety"

Here are some simple tools that have been very effective for me in conquering fear and anxiety:

-Meditate day and night with GOD - Creator and controller of this entire Universe.
-LOVE
-White Sage
-Frankincense Incense
-Lavender Candle
-Classical, Relaxing Music
-Hyssop Tea
-Take a walk-in nature
-Deep Breathing
-Speak daily positive affirmations out loud.
-Surround yourself with positive and loving people.

It's a process. Every Individual is different. Ask and seek your Higher Power for direction to CONQUER fear and anxiety! It's all in the mind.

"Conquer Fear and Anxiety"

Notes:

Insight 9:

"Turn the TV Off"

"Your *Home* space should be used for relaxation and freedom from the outside world. Your family will appreciate a positive environment and this is an easy tool to *not* use, to keep the heavy flow of negative energy out of your *Home*. In my experience, television is connected to a huge energy field. It is a telecommunication medium for transmitting and receiving moving images with or without accompanying sound.

FEAR: False Evidence Appearing Real.

Your *Home* should be a RELAXED atmosphere for your family and friends to be able to come and fellowship and shower love upon one another; the television is a contradictory source of energy to your loved one's experience."

~ Healing Cosmetologist

In other words, TURN the TV OFF and play some RELAXING MUSIC!

Music SOOTHES the Soul!

"Turn the TV Off!"

Notes:

Insight 10:

"Strong and Independent"

Well, let's define the words Strong and Independent: Strong: one who exerts power; Independent: one not controlled by others.

Growing up as a strong independent young woman came from having a very strong provider and father figure. I make no apologies for my strength; yet, I believe there is a level of balance with strength as a woman that occurs with maturity and wisdom. My independence and strength was necessary for the trial and errors in my life. Being blessed with a mother who loves me unconditionally is what has taught me love, balance, peace and how to prepare for becoming a Queen.

As a woman of African American and Native Indian descent, I have awakened to my truest self. My childhood was the beginning of the creation of self. The major influences while growing up (parents, teachers, school, and church) created many ideas of identity of who I should become. Influences are nothing more than the sharing and teaching of experiences and opinions of their life story.

As we mature, we begin to separate the positive from the negative influences. We begin to absorb the teachings that have become effective in our lives positively and we begin to create and mold into what God has purposed US to become. The outcome is for us to become better than our influences so that the next generation can learn from our mistakes and create a much better world.

We all have a story. We all have experiences. Our upbringing, teachings, beliefs, opinions, ideas, comprehension, and experiences vary based on the response of the outcome. The outcome is for a purpose, there's a plan for every situation. Earth is a classroom. The plan is to learn from our mistakes so that we may experience blissful living. Seeking to love is the greatest lesson of all!!

God has gifted me with the responsibility of being a mother. As a strong black beautiful woman-motherhood has softened the "edges" of being "strong" and "independent".

Operating as a responsible, nurturing mother, allows my strength to shine as a Queen. Having "independence" stripped for such a time as this has created a desire within to become totally dependent upon God. Being dependent upon God gives the word "independence" a new meaning. There is a new appreciation for being strong AND independent!

Lesson learned for me as an individual spirit with an individual purpose: In order to operate fully and successfully in one's life purpose, one must become TOTALLY dependent upon God, the Creator of ALL, Almighty Divine! As you begin to TRUST, BELIEVE, and MOVE toward your heart's desire - heaven on earth becomes a reality. Study and seek knowledge about who you are, where you come from, and why you are the way you are. Operating in who you desire to become without fear reverses the chains of mental slavery. Being transparent is the new freedom! Oh, what a delight to experience such freedom!

"Strong and Independent"

Notes:

Insight 11:

"Mother, the Nurturer"

About three years ago, GOD spoke to me:

"Baby girl, close down the Salon, worry not of ANY finances. You and your children WILL be cared for during this transition. I will return to you 100-fold of blessings and favor upon you and your children and children's children, generational favor will be upon you…if only you would POSITION yourself as a FULL-TIME Mother and begin writing books of your knowledge so that you will be Spiritually, Financially, Mentally, Emotionally, and Physically successful by way of your

THOUGHTS. Intellectual Property is the Highest Commodity."

~ *Healing Cosmetologist*

And because of my obedience to the Almighty DIVINE GOD of the UNIVERSE who rules and super rules, His WORD is TRUE!! So here it is, manifested into physical form...

"Mother, the Nurturer."

CHILDREN are GOD-given GIFTS, they are your reasons for being and provide inspiration of why we exist! Children keep you grounded. Children are your power base. The responsibility of parenting allows one to experience and operate unconditional love.

The responsibility of a mother is to TEACH and NURTURE these divine beings GOD has put you in charge of. As time-consuming as children are, children need to be INSPIRED and ENCOURAGED at ALL times. What is the Sacrifice? YOUR TIME, not material things.

Mothers have the POWER to feed into their children's EXPANDED powers. This POWER dwells within their SPIRIT. A Mother has the POWER to POUR into her children when their SPIRIT is in need of LIGHT. Woman is the sub-conscious mind of GOD, which means she has access to the divine thoughts of GOD without reasoning. Children nowadays come here with a KNOWING that they are DESTINED to be GREAT. Mothers are their FIRST teacher.

So, you asked, "How did you get to a place to fully trust God and move forward toward the words He had spoken to you?"

Well, there were three questions that arose during this transition for me to answer:

- What am I willing to sacrifice for the betterment of my children's future?

- What am I willing to do to live a blissful life?

- What was I willing to do to help others to learn this type of success?

Answers:

As a sacrifice, I gave up the material life that I had acquired, my independence, my business, my physical desires (which has been the MOST challenging at times and still is), and even acquaintances in my life that were not for my good.

Because of the chaotic times that we currently live in, God was preparing me to become more available to my Children and pour into them about the spirit of discernment. Children NEED and YEARN LOVE, SUPPORT, and SPIRITUAL nurturing at ALL times. In order to pour these things into my children and be available to them at ALL times, I had to decrease the energy given toward a job and people who had nothing to offer toward my greatness and become available to my Children so they could FEED off on my energy!!

To have the ENERGY to pour and attend to your children's spiritual, mental, and physical needs, one MUST be in alignment with the DIVINE GOD to be able to HEAR his directions for your life.

This prayer has been very effective for me during this transition:

"Lord keep me safe from temptation, that pulls at my emotions and my physical needs that call out to my sense of what I deserve and what I have the right to feel and enjoy!"

I send love and light to ALL MOTHERS!! RISE and take your POSITION!

"Mother, the Nurturer"

Notes:

Insight 12:

"Inner Peace"

"The sense of touch has a high frequency of energy that affects a person's whole entire aura (the energy that surrounds a person). Any external source of positive energy can cause you to 'feel' love, joy, and peace; while negative energy can cause you to 'feel' depressed, angry, or fearful.

Entities (spirits) are very easy to pick up from anywhere; they latch onto us when we become very vulnerable negatively and open as a weakened Spirit.

A weakened Spirit is open to negative forces, especially if the physical being is not in control of their OWN mind; for that is where the enemy has the ability to control you.

When we are feeling low, our vibrations are lower and we become easy targets for negative forces. When we are happy, our vibrations are higher, and we are easy targets for positive forces.

When vibrations rise with positive vibrations, you will begin to desire happiness, love, joy, and peace. A continuation of this practice will ignite this gift of discernment and you will begin to differentiate between energy frequency changes; positive vs negative.

This is why it is important to feed (read, apply and practice with understanding), your Spirit with: The Word of God, Speak Positive Affirmations out loud, Practice Meditation daily and ignite the Gift of Discernment- in order to ward off negative surrounding seen and unseen Entities."

~Healing Cosmetologist

And THIS is the beginning of Manifesting "INNER PEACE".

"Inner Peace"

Notes:

In Conclusion

"Deepening My Spirituality: When I desired a deeper relationship with the Divine and all that encompasses His Universe; spiritual gifting's\higher dimensional dwellings, Spirituality began to find ME."

~ *Healing Cosmetologist*

Insight is a book of short stories that offers insight on how to awaken one's consciousness. Knowledge is power!

To awaken the consciousness, I use the Chakra System as the main source of information. The word Chakra represents energy within the physical body. The body is made up of blood, muscles, bones, organs, and energy. Energy is the strength to sustain spiritual, physical, and mental ability. Allow me to give you a visual:

There are seven main chakras —energy spaces within the body:

- The Root Chakra is located at the base of the spine or where your reproductive organs dwell.
- The Sacral Chakra is located at the belly button.
- The Solar Plexus is located at the core of the body, stomach area.
- The Heart Chakra is in the center of the chest, where the heart is located.
- The Throat Chakra is located at the center of the throat.
- The Third Eye Chakra dwells in between the eyes, at the forehead.
- The Crown Chakra is located at the top of the head.

Each energy space represents an emotion. Because energy sustains mental activity, when it's ignited or awakened, it has the power to expand the thinking of a human being. This is key to releasing "slave" mentality. Slave: one who obeys another person's thoughts and beliefs. An awakening allows one to trust their own inner voice and spirit.

We are all created in the image of the Creator of the Universe, which means we have the power to create. When one has a one-track mind, and follows the thinking of the masses or its slave master, their way of thinking stays inside the box. Creation of greatness is based on an individual's thought which dwells outside the box and forms new ideas and thoughts. Creation of self within an individual's spirit, not its slave master's. Aligning the energy centers of the body (Chakra) to the main source of the Creator ignites one's reason of being, reason of why you were created, and your life's purpose. Your life purpose cannot be defined by anyone but yourself. The Seven Chakras, energy source within the body, is related to the Seven Churches in the "Book of Revelation". The body of Christ is YOU… not a building.

Allow me to share my insight regarding the body of Christ and the connection to the Third Eye Chakra:

Your Third Eye (energy space between your eyes) is a record of emotions you've experienced throughout your life. The Third Eye Chakra functions with the pituitary gland in the brain; it's the MASTER gland of the body.

When this center is kept active, your spoken word will always shed more light on a situation which is the main center for higher perceptions.

The pituitary gland produces a hormone that affects the modulation of wake/sleep patterns.

Sodium fluoride is in our water supply, food, and soda. An over consumption of sodium fluoride can have a negative effect of the pituitary gland. It functions as a substance, which has the ability to dumb one's thinking.

The Third Eye energy space is recognized as the "seat of the soul". If you take away the "seat of the soul", this disconnects our oneness with God and the power of our source and our spirituality.

Third Eye Chakra ~ Perception, INSIGHT, Super-consciousness, ~ Related to Intuition

In the body, this energy space is located at the forehead.

Perception is the ability to become aware of the six senses. Perception interprets one's mind-set. The Superconscious Mind is the highest level of thought in the human brain.

Christ Consciousness- having the mindset of Christ.

Mastering Meditation and Concentration allows one to activate this energy.

This energy space represents the realization that life's difficulties are illusions through which we can grow and expand our consciousness.

This energy space, when activated, enhances intellectual and intuitive abilities.

A disciplined mind has the ability to unite the five senses which will ignite the sixth sense, which is intuition.

Here's a mantra that will help you tune into your inner self to clear your Third Eye Chakra:

"Because God is the Creator of all and I trust and obey His will, I ask God to remove any fear and doubts about the ability to create my future. What I speak will manifest. I speak out-loud, "I am of greatness" and my future will become of greatness. Because I am under the authority of God, my vision is aligned with His vision. This vision I see is good, full of love, joy, peace and prosperity. Ase! (and so it is)

Finally, it all makes sense to ME! The Bible is to be read so that it applies to MY daily life, something that I can relate to.

During my studies in Metaphysics, I discovered this understanding: The Bible is mystical; its writing is made up of symbols that have meanings beyond what has been written. Growing up in the Baptist Church there was always something missing. It wasn't clear to me what exactly the Bible was speaking about until I spoke with purpose to the Creator, "There's got to be more than what I've been taught. God show me more of you."

Metaphysics is where I found the answer. Metaphysics is the study of the mind, the philosophy explaining the real nature of the state of being. This philosophy ignited something within me, a knowing that was always there.

This opens the understanding of one's life purpose. When you are walking in your life's purpose, all needs will be met and to survive becomes everlasting. You will no longer walk in the minds of the masses, you will become set apart, and peculiar. You will find that you operate as your own unique being—the one that God has created you to be.

This is freeing and this is why the book *Insight* has been created.

I pray you have Enjoyed this reading and have become Enlightened!

In Conclusion

Notes:

About the Author

Nicole Lee

Author, Counsel to the Entrepreneur and Visionary with advanced knowledge of Universal Law coupled with business success strategies, personal growth, and spiritual tools used for enhancing one's life towards bliss.

Nicole Lee Publications:

-Healing Cosmetologist

- Insight

-Emotional Remedies Calendar

- How to Eradicate Emotional Paralysis- Guide for Single Moms

-How to Write and Publish My Own Book

-Healing Beauty

-Wisdom of a Queen

-Don't Touch My Hair!

-Savagery

-How to Eradicate Fear- A Guide for Everybody

Visit Nicole Online:

Website:
-www.NicoleLee.me
-www.WarriorMoms.us

LinkedIn: Nicole Lee and Healing In Cosmetology Group

Google Business:
Counsel to the Entrepreneur, LLC

www.ingramcontent.com/pod-product-compliance
Lightning Source LLC
Chambersburg PA
CBHW022129280326
41933CB00007B/603